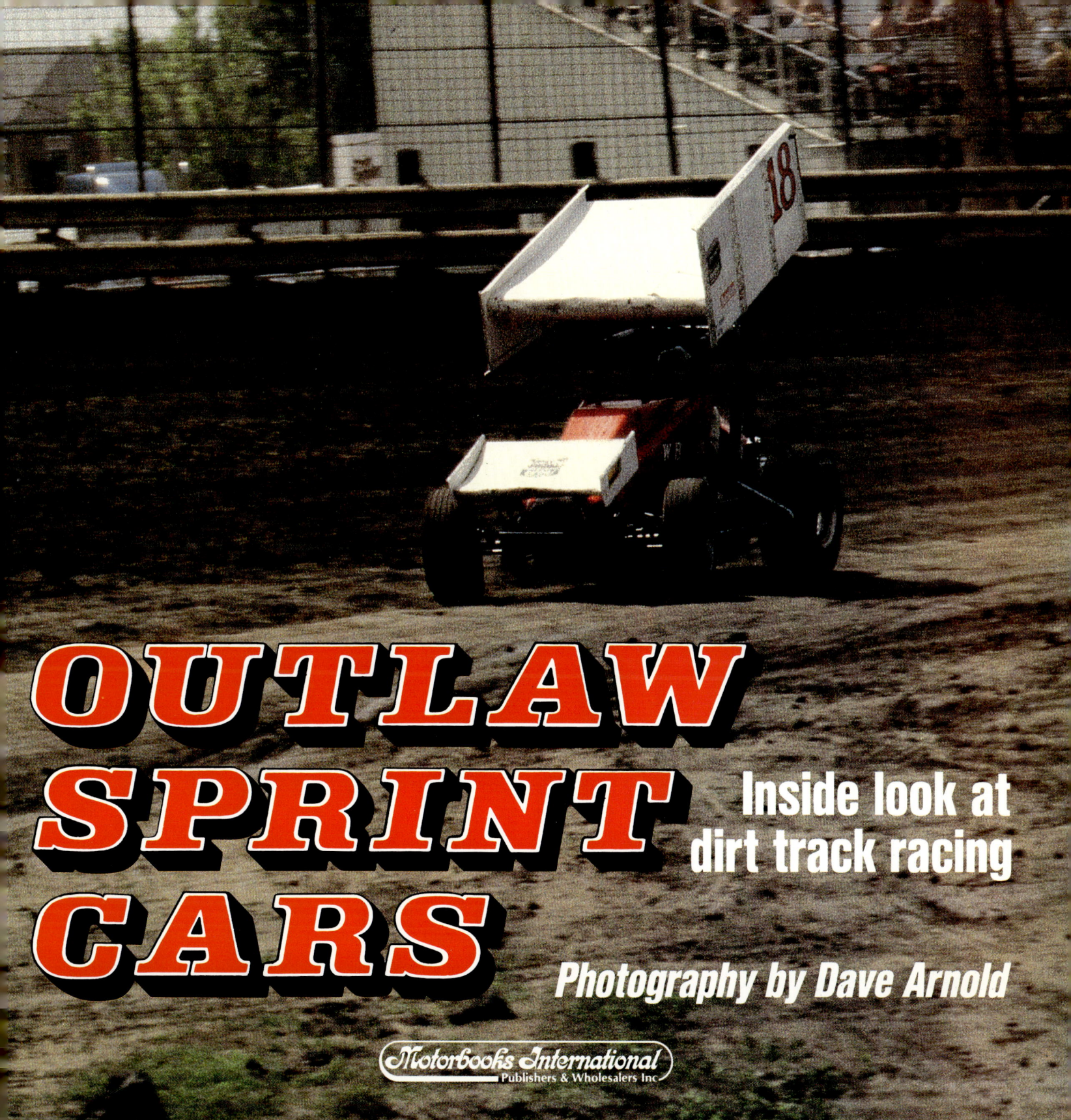

First published in 1987 by Motorbooks International Publishers & Wholesalers Inc, PO Box 2, 729 Prospect Avenue, Osceola, WI 54020 USA

© Dave Arnold, 1987

All rights reserved. With the exception of quoting brief passages for the purposes of review no part of this publication may be reproduced without prior written permission from the publisher

Motorbooks International is a certified trademark, registered with the United States Patent Office

Printed and bound in Hong Kong

The information in this book is true and complete to the best of our knowledge. All recommendations are made without any guarantee on the part of the author or publisher, who also disclaim any liability incurred in connection with the use of this data or specific details

We recognize that World of Outlaws and other associated names are the property of that organization. We gratefully use them with permission. This is not an official publication of the World of Outlaws, Inc.

Motorbooks International books are also available at discounts in bulk quantity for industrial or sales-promotional use. For details write to Special Sales Manager at the Publisher's address.

Library of Congress Cataloging-in-Publication Data

Arnold, Dave
  Outlaw sprint cars.

       1. Sprint cars—History. 2. Automobile racing—
History. I. Title.
GV1029.9.S67A76 1987796.7'287-1527
ISBN 0-87938-243-0

Front cover photo by Phil Dullinger.

Dedication

To my father, Orie Arnold, who first took me to see sprinters and midgets at the old Biglow Field in Grand Rapids, Michigan.

On the cover

Robby Unser, son of two-time national champion Bobby Unser drifting out of turn two at Knoxville in preparation for the dash to turn three. The car is a Ford-powered Challenger.

Title page

Two clearly different lines through turn one at Knoxville. Who would dare say one is more correct than the other? Some of the most fascinating sprint racing occurs when two closely competitive cars use totally different portions of the track; one roaring wide open high on the cushion and the other being finessed tightly around the corners as low as possible.

Half title

Apple pie, motherhood and the American flag in the Midwest.

Right

What can be better than a close-up trackside seat, soft summer breezes, a cold brew in your hand and the anticipation of an evening watching the World of Outlaws?

Acknowledgements

The task of collecting photos, facts and information for this book was one of the most enjoyable undertakings I've attempted in a long time. People who made this project a pleasure and to whom I owe a big thank you include: Bob Trostle, Trostle Racing, Inc.; Bob Westphal, Wesmar Racing Engines; Ron Shaver, Shaver Racing Engines; Butch Evans, Speedway Airflow Enterprises; Glen Sander, Sander Engineeering; P.J. Lauritzen, Goodyear Tire Co.; Lyle Marsh, Marsh Racing Tires; and Ralph Capitani, Race Director, Knoxville Raceway.

Contents

Preface	6
Introduction	7
Engines	8
Suspensions	20
Tires	36
Wings	48
Signs	60
Rigs	70
Manufacturers	78
Personalities	90
Accidents	100
On track	108

Preface

The music world has Dixieland, international cuisine has the hamburger and automobile racing has the dirt track sprint car. Just as Dixieland and the hamburger are uniquely American contributions to their respective fields, so too is the sprinter.

Born of depression era economics and nurtured on the dusty, small-town tracks of the Midwest and East Coast fair circuits, these cars developed building formulas, driving requirements, terminology and a folklore distinct from the rest of the motor racing world. Sprint car racing sprouted, flourished and, to this day, continues almost as if it were an island unto itself. During the fifties and sixties it was the American training ground for the step up to Indy-type cars, and for some like the incredible A. J. Foyt and the multi-talented Mario Andretti, the beginning of very successful careers in international-level competition.

Today, however, sprint car racing no longer seems to be just a stepping stone to other forms of racing. In fact, Formula One, CART/USAC and other professionals often emerge from the road racing circuits with extensive prior training from formal driving schools in the United States and Europe. Another reason is that sprint car drivers and other personnel no longer see it as such.

Recent years have seen a maturing of this form of racing. Race attendance has increased dramatically, prize money has grown geometrically, racing equipment has become more sophisticated and competition has intensified. It's not uncommon nowdays for the winner of a major event such as the Nationals in Knoxville, Iowa, to earn more than even the third-place finisher in such a highly publicized race as the Pocono 500.

Many of sprint racing's top names give but a passing thought to other forms of motor competition. In fact, American dirt track sprint car racing just might be the top of the ladder for a whole family of distinctly American racing classes, from the simplest jalopy/stocker cars through various modifieds to the incredibly engineered and competitive supermodifieds and midgets.

With these thoughts in mind, let's take an up-close look at the sprint car, the focal point of this uniquely American brand of motor racing. Let's examine its major components, look at some racing action and spot a few of its key personnel.

Introduction

Sprint car racing began in the early twenties for a variety of reasons. One of the more important ones was the ready availability and low cost of the four-cylinder Ford Model T engine. By 1928, and the advent of the slightly larger Ford Model A engine, an automotive performance aftermarket had developed into full bloom. With a wide range of hop-up and performance equipment available, the dowdy Ford four-banger could be turned into a raging terror capable of beating the best that Miller and other specialty builders could produce. As competition increased, the stock-block Ford engine was eventually pushed to its limit. With the addition of aftermarket components it became as complex and therefore as expensive as purpose-built racing motors.

The thirties and forties saw the rise of specialty engines in sprinters, with the famous Offenhauser eventually moving to the head of the pack.

A year of major significance was 1956 because another American automobile manufacturer (this time it was Chevrolet) produced a stock engine destined to put the specialty racing engine back on the shelf. As with the early Ford Model T and A engines, a high-performance aftermarket quickly developed for the new small-block V-8.

By the early sixties, the Offenhauser was running for its life on American racetracks, very often unsuccessfully. The stock-block engine had returned with a vengeance. Almost anyone could buy a Chevy block from the local salvage yard, purchase sophisticated high-quality performance components, spend a little money at a competent machine shop and bolt together an engine capable of the power and performance that had been available a short ten years earlier from only the world's most expensive designers and builders.

Thus emerged the modern sprint car engine from the small-block V-8 produced by Chevrolet. In reality, though, the modern sprinter engine, while referred to as being "Chevy-based," "small-block" and so on is no more stock than the thirties four-cylinder Model A Ford engine with its extensive aftermarket components. From its dry-sump oil pan to its alcohol injectors, today's sprint engine is a combination of the best possible components from a host of aftermarket suppliers, and its horsepower and cost reflect that.

Engines

The king of the sprint car circuit is the Chevrolet-based 400 cubic inch, four-bolt main bearing small-block V-8 engine. The World of Outlaws, an organization known for the simplicity and paucity of its rules, states that engines run under its jurisdiction will not exceed 410 cubic inches, will not be allowed turbo- or superchargers and cannot use any additives such as nitromethane or nitrous oxide in the standard, pure methanol fuel. Aluminum blocks are typically from Donovan or Rodeck, while heads are generally by Brownfield, Brodix or Dart. Which vender's parts go into the block, how passages are ported, tolerances fitted and adjustments made are all part of the dark science practiced by such builders as Westphal, Shaver, Gerte and a host of others. Most racers agree the standard 650 hp engine will cost approximately $21,000 and will run about fourteen nights of racing before needing a $3,000 rebuild. Very often, with proper rebuilds, it will last an entire season. A 730 hp higher-output engine will cost about $1,000 more, run seven to ten nights before needing a rebuild and will be more likely to fail because of high rpm which generate extra horsepower but also overtax the somewhat modest bearing surfaces inherent in the Chevy stock-block-based design. Standard-horsepower engines are typically run at 6700 to 7000 rpm while higher-output versions are turned at 7500 to 7600, with some run at 7800 rpm.

The Ford engine has recently joined (rejoined) the sprint car circuit with an aluminum aftermarket design based on the 351 Windsor block. Proponents and concerned Chevy people note this new engine with its larger bearing surfaces, heavier bottom-end strength and larger bottom-end clearances apparently has good performance potential. Its only limitations seem to be the lack of developmental momentum possesed by the Chevy crowd and its wider block which will not fit into the standard chassis designed for the Chevy unit.

Methanol is the fuel of choice for a majority of sprint car events, and certainly for the World of Outlaws. Blown engines and excessive repair costs are the primary reasons for the Outlaws opting for methanol (nitromethane is the usual power-producing additive that caused the increased expenses). The typical sprinter will burn thirty to forty gallons of fuel in a thirty-lap race for a one to 1 ½ mile-per-gallon average. Racing methanol costs approximately $2 per gallon and produces a wonderfully pungent, sweet smell and exciting blue exhaust header flame when burned in the rich mixture ratios demanded by racing engines.

Direct port injection. The four black hoses running to brass fittings in this photo are a relatively recent development designed to increase horsepower. They are fuel-injector lines typically run to the air horns on a conventional fuel-injection system, but in this case they were removed and plumbed directly through the head, entering the intake port just upstream from the valve head. The object is to increase airflow through the air horn and not take up valuable air space or create a turbulent flow high up in the air horn by injecting fuel at that point. Dyno tests normally show a 25 hp increase with this installation.

The dial just to the right of the steering wheel is a device drivers use during a race to change fuel-injection jet settings. Most sprint car injection systems are the low-pressure/constant-flow type with provision for excess fuel to be returned to the fuel tank. Various jet sizes determine the rate at which fuel can flow back to the tank, with the remaining flow going to the cylinders. By adjusting the dial, a driver can richen a lean, hot-running engine while in competition. Often, drivers will select a rich setting to quickly cool a hot engine during a temporary yellow-flag situation, returning the setting to a lean position for maximum performance when the green flag appears. Engine builders are leery of this practice since misselection of a setting, not unlikely even under a yellow flag, can quickly result in serious engine damage.

Hiding down low in the cockpit are the power steering and fuel pumps. These units receive their power drive from the engine's camshaft. Note the knee pads in the upper portion of the picture and the shielded drive shaft which runs between the driver's legs.

Nestled between the engine block and the radiator is the dry-sump oil pump generally found on higher-performance sprinter engines. The typical sprinter carries a three-gallon oil tank and does not use any form of oil cooler, due to the short duration of sprint car races. These pumps with associated components can cost from $700 to $800, seemingly a lot to pay for an oil pump, until you remember its job is to lubricate and protect an engine worth as much as $21,000.

Suspensions

Adjustable friction shocks and transverse leaf springs—rear suspension, from about 1930.

Over $1,700 worth of torsion bars. At $115 each and with a life span of twenty to twenty-five races, torsion bars are definitely an expensive consumable in sprint car racing. Experienced mechanics and drivers agree that torsion bars seldom break or fatigue to the point of not being able to properly support a car. Rather, right from the very first jolt it absorbs, a bar gradually requires more and more response time to properly reposition a chassis. This degradation occurs so slowly that it is seldom noticeable. If not taken into consideration, the driver and crew, unhappy with a car's performance, may begin to adjust other variables such as wing settings or tire pressure, in an attempt to correct a handling problem. When they do finally install new bars, the other adjustments may well then be incorrect.

Tires, torsion bars and shocks are the basic tools of a skilled mechanic assigned the task of getting a car around a dirt track in the shortest possible time. A spare front axle hangs from the ceiling of this trailering rig, just in case it's needed.

Close-up of the left rear axle on a Gambler chassis showing the highly ventilated brake disc and caliper mechanism. Brakes are typically found on both front wheels and inboard on the left rear axle. One is sufficient on a sprinter's rear end, due to the nondifferential feature of the third member.

Next page
Doesn't look quite so mean and imposing without those giant rear tires, does it? This scene is very typical of sprint tracks throughout the nation—the cars race in the dirt and they are fixed, maintained and repaired in the dirt. It's not uncommon to see open gearboxes and intricate fuel-injection components being worked on in this environment. Experienced mechanics routinely keep these sophisticated components running properly with little effect from dirt on the track and in the pits.

The modern sprinter is normally sprung by four transversely mounted torsion bars. Here we see the left front corner of a Nance chassis. The large end of the aluminum torsion arm (with the lightening holes) is splined to one end of a torsion bar. The narrow end of the torsion arm rides on the front axle, inputing twist to the torsion bar as the axle moves up and down. The opposite end of the torsion bar, on the other side of the car, is splined to a short arm called a torsion stop, which rides against a frame-member, preloading the torsion bar and holding that end motionless so the bar can absorb twist.

One more look at torsion bars, this time on the front end of a RaceKraft chassis. Most important here is the fact these bars are hollow, and are claimed to result in a faster reaction time with no center mass to slow up twisting motion, and superior heat treating due to accessibility of more surface area. A process very similar to drilling a rifle barrel is used to drill hollow torsion bars. While bars are interchangeable from corner to corner, most mechanics mark them to be run on one corner only and seldom put a bar in a position where it is twisted in the opposite direction. This results in even faster deterioration of reaction time.

Previous page
This photo shows the right rear of a Gambler chassis. The heavy aluminum torsion arm extending backward from the axle is splined to a transversely mounted torsion bar. Immediately behind the torsion arm is the torsion stop, which locks the torsion bar for the left wheel in position allowing the bar to absorb twist. Why torsion bars rather than coil springs? While there are somewhat persuasive technical arguments in favor of bars, many chassis builders tend to feel it's more of a psychological issue for drivers: Bars are "state of the art," coil springs are "old fashioned."

Definitely an old-style front suspension, yet seen in competition at Knoxville in 1986! If front coil springs went out of style in the late seventies, then front leaf springs dropped from favor in the *early* seventies. There are proponents who claim transversely mounted leaf springs are ideal for sprint car application because they are properly positioned to work the bumps as a car drifts sideways, the attitude in which sprinters spend a great deal of their time.

One of the more recent developments in sprint car suspension comes from the Challenger company. This mechanism consists of a coil spring wrapped around a shock absorber. It's mounted to the car's frame on top, and to a boxlike structure on the bottom, which is then attached to the rear end. Challenger claims this device frees the rear suspension from binding problems inherent in the traditional design, allowing the rear tires better traction. One thing for certain, it does further complicate an already cramped sprint car cockpit!

Sparkling in the sun awaiting a team in immediate need is $6,000 worth of quick-change rear end. Manufactured by Winters Performance Products, these high-precision units must absorb tremendous shock loads created by screaming engines, sticky tires and rutted tracks. Built with aluminum or magnesium cases and aluminum axle shafts (yes, aluminum) and weighing approximately 110 pounds, a rear end unit should be virtually trouble-free. The most likely source of failure will be the ring-and-pinion gears, which will not be a problem if changed every twenty to thirty evenings of racing.

Tires

36

The way it was: knobbies in the back and treads in the front, the same size on all four corners; spidery-looking spoked wheels; high-pressure tires with innertubes; and a roll center just slightly below those low-running clouds.

Next page

The modern sprinter: grooved slicks; low-pressure tires with no tubes; frequently a different size tire on each corner; aluminum, steel or carbon fiber wheels. It's an automobile which, when sitting still in race-ready condition, looks as if it has a twisted frame and needs some serious chassis work.

Front tires on a sprinter normally carry the most pressure, with the left front carrying about 10 psi and the right front carrying up to a bead-bursting 12 psi! Manufacturers don't produce enough incremental sizes in front tires to provide for reasonable stagger possibilities, so tires must be used which are slightly off-standard sizes. Size differences can also be obtained by inflating a tire to the 50 psi range and allowing it to sit for twenty-four hours. This will frequently stretch the materials enough to result in the desired change.

Tire stagger, especially at the rear, is, in most mechanics' and drivers' minds, the single most important tire-related factor in getting a car around a track fast—even moreso than tire compound. First experimented with in the mid-sixties, stagger is usually discussed in terms of inches of roll-out or inches of tire circumference. It is altered in a sprinter by changing the left rear tire size. Manufacturers typically produce six different roll-out sizes for left rear tires, ranging in two-inch increments from eighty-eight to ninety-eight inches. They produce these sizes in a very limited number of hardness compounds. The right rear tire, on the other hand (the tire that carries a majority of the load and force), is typically produced in very few roll-out sizes but in a good variety of hardness compounds. So, stagger is altered by changing tire roll-out on the left rear, and compound is altered by changing the right rear.

Here is a sprinter with a shredded left rear. Tire company representatives claim ninety-nine percent of sprint car tire failures are due to improper tire pressure; that is, tires that are underinflated rather than overinflated. Typical tire pressures for winged sprinters range from 6 to 10 psi on the right rear and 3 to 6 psi on the left rear. The frequent tendency to want to run low pressures to improve traction many times results in one of two problems: Either a tire sidewall becomes so distorted in attempting to contain 700 hp that the tire fabric is actually torn apart, or the distortion allows the wheel rim to ride on the sidewall, further stressing it and possibly even cutting the surface.

Sprint cars appear to be hard, strong and very tough vehicles—until you take a closer look at the tires, especially the rear tires. The rear tires on a sprinter feel more like a thick-skinned balloon or a beach toy than a hard-surfaced passenger-car tire. Low pressure coupled with very soft compound results in a tread surface easy to deflect either with a finger or a fist. The compound is amazingly soft, so soft it feels as though you could tear it with your fingernails. It seems impossible that these compliant bags of air can absorb 700 screaming horsepower as a car drifts sideways through corners at over 100 mph, lurching over ridges, slamming into ruts and shattering track surfaces. Bob Trostle and Earl Wagner were the first to try wide, low-pressure tires in 1968, when Trostle mounted grooved Goodyear drag racing tires on his house car. The effect was so positive that the car won features three weeks in a row at Knoxville. Photos of the tires deflecting in the corners (no beadlocks were used in those days) were so frightening that driver Wagner and owner Trostle decided there had to be a safer way to win races and put the idea aside for future consideration.

The normal sprinter enters a race with nearly $500 worth of tires in three different sizes, utilizing three different hardness compounds and running four different tire pressures. The more affluent teams running an evening of high prize money races will often run a soft compound for qualifying, a medium compound for heat races and a hard compound for the feature race, depending on the changing track conditions as the evening wears on. Pressures, compound hardness and stagger are the three major variables a mechanic works with when practicing the black art of hooking a car up to the track. A common practice of most teams, depending on the track, is grooving tires to help with traction or heat rejection. (Each mechanic has different thoughts on the subject.) In this photo a tire is being "buttoned out," a technique designed to help the tread lose heat.

There are few examples of space-age materials being used in sprint car racing. One area where this has taken place, though, is in the use of carbon fiber in rear wheel construction. The benefits are claimed to be fifty percent weight reduction and fifty percent cost reduction over the normally priced ($280) aluminum wheel. Additionally, carbon fiber wheels are claimed to absorb shock loads better than aluminum wheels. This feature takes substantial loads off a sprinter's rear end, loads which are encountered during jolting sideways drifts, in bumping and in accidents.

Wings

48

The addition of wings to the dirt track sprinter has been one of the more significant and controversial changes during recent decades. A fairly complex structure, it consists of a section like a small aircraft wing turned upside-down and mounted above the car's roll cage on a manual or hydraulically actuated mechanism. The side plates are of particular significance, since a sprinter spends much of its time traveling sideways. The plate on the left-hand side of this wing (right-hand side of the picture) extends above the wing, preventing air from slipping off the top edge of the wing and forcing it to flow from front to rear as the car drifts sideways through a corner. The plate on the right side extends primarily below the wing, preventing air from getting underneath the wing from the side, which would ruin the desired front-to-rear airflow and result in loss of desired downward force.

Shown here, waiting to be mounted, is the underside of a wing with its attaching brackets and manually adjustable trailing edge (at the top). The trailing edge adjustment and the multiple positioning of the wing on the roll cage give the driver and mechanic a wide latitude of adjustment. Properly rigged at an approximate twelve-degree angle of attack, the top wing of a sprint car will generate approximately 600 pounds of downforce, with about 100 to 150 pounds of aerodynamic drag at 100 mph. In the turns, when the wing is of primary benefit to a sprinter, there will be about 1,000 pounds of force transmitted to the car, due to the downforce of the front-to-back airflow over the wing and the side loads on the end plates.

No, this is not an after-the-accident shot, but rather a sprint car full of innovations; two are the front and top wings. Theoretically, both are canted and angled to take better advantage of airflow while drifting through turns. At the time of this photo, test results appeared inconclusive, possibly because of numerous other innovations, which cloud one's understanding of wing performance.

Previous page
Decried by car owners as too expensive at $450 for the large wing and $80 for the nose unit, the $500 to $600 cost of these aerodynamic devices is actually about the cheapest pieces of speed equipment on a sprinter. The nose wing normally generates about sixty pounds of downforce and is used primarily as a means of fine tuning a car's balance. The World of Outlaws specifies a maximum top wing size of twenty-five square feet and a front wing size of six square feet.

The lever to the left of the steering wheel is the cockpit control used by the driver to adjust the top wing positions. This mechanism is hydraulic and is driven by the power steering pump. It was first developed and used in 1984 by car owner Karl Kinser.

The carriage assembly, seen here with the top wing removed, is controlled by the cockpit lever. The two front supports remain fixed, while the two back supports pivot at their mountings on the roll cage. As the wing is moved backward, the trailing edge is forced upward, resulting in an increased angle of attack (more downward pressure on the car) as well as a transfer of downforce from front to rear wheels.

A graphic example of aerodynamic loads on wing surfaces is this side plate, which has broken loose and spills air over the side when the sprinter is in mid-turn. Since side plates absorb the heaviest loads in turns, failure at this point will change car handling dramatically.

Signs

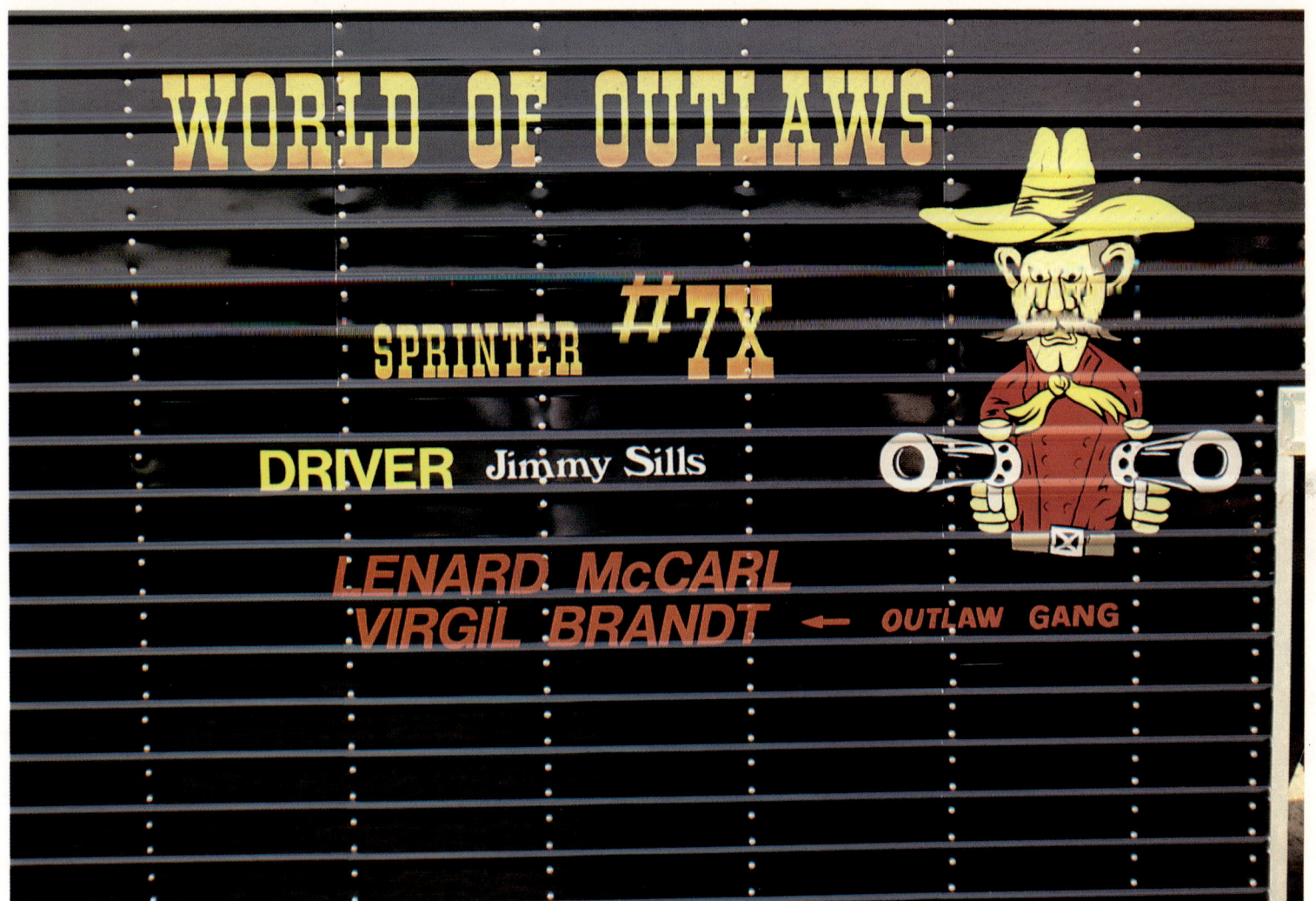

When you have $75,000 invested in race equipment and nearly as much in a tow rig, why not spend a few bucks more and fill the empty surfaces with neat graphics to promote yourself and your cause? Bright colors, fancy paint jobs and interesting messages abound in the world of sprint car racing.

A couple of dashboard reminders, just in case a driver begins to wonder why he is out there driving an open-wheel car sideways at 100 mph. Note these two cars, like most others, carry minimal instrumentation. Especially interesting is the fact few sprinters use a tachometer. The large variety of rear end gears and rear tire sizes allows a mechanic to very closely tailor engine rpm to any track length, thus negating the need for a tach.

Where would the world be without T-shirt graphics to promote causes and identify egos? This spectator at Knoxville is as much a part of the show as the cars, drivers and mechanics.

Dirt track racing, like other sports, has developed its own set of cliches and humor to tickle the funny bone. In this case, there seems to be competition from the hard track people.

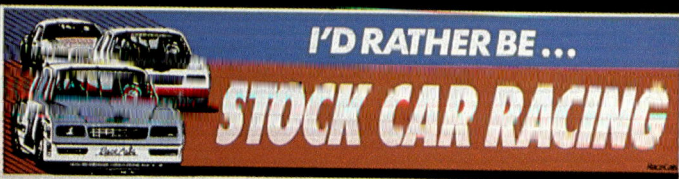

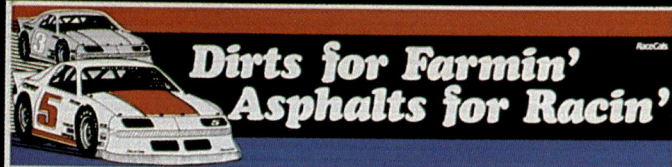
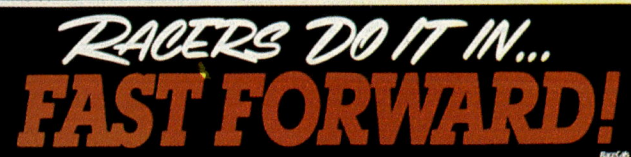
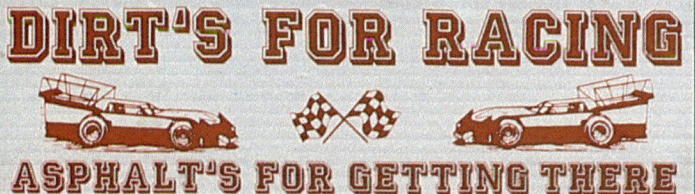

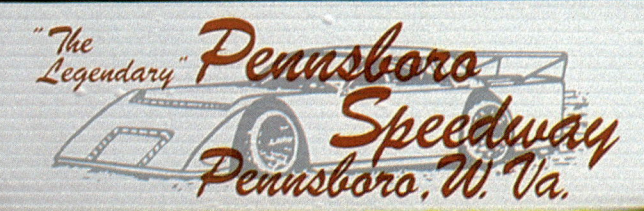

With twice-a-week racing virtually all over the nation from February through November, with organizations such as the World of Outlaws, the circuit can become a long, grueling and obviously lonesome road to follow. Notice this sign doesn't mention a need for mechanical skills or proven race experience.

Hoosier
RACING TIRE

RACERS GO IN DEEPER AND COME OUT HARDER

Rigs

Previous page
Trailering rigs come in all types and sizes. This number 10N Nance-chassis car was Terry Grey's mount during his 1986 campaign and illustrates one way to go racing on a limited budget.

Complete with a well-outfitted workshop, spare components, nightlights and even wood paneling, this rig exemplifies a fairly common approach to transporting a sprinter around the dozens of tracks and across the thousands of miles an Outlaw team covers during a summer of competition.

Large trailers provide plenty of room for spare parts and equipment often needed on short notice: tires, wheels, axles and, would you believe, forty sets of gears for a sprinter's quick-change rear end! Such a large selection of gear sets is quite common, allowing a team, in combination with different tire sizes, to almost perfectly tune an engine's rpm for maximum performance on tracks ranging in size from one-fifth mile to one mile.

Next page
Racing engines and chassis are expensive; and tires, wings and so on all add to the cost of racing. When you're touring the circuit in a rig like this, probably with a couple of spare engines inside, you're making a statement about your financial ability to race. Too bad great-looking rigs don't automatically guarantee great-performing sprinters inside!

Manufacturers

Bob Trostle Racing, Inc., Des Moines, Iowa. Trostle has produced approximately 380 chassis during his nearly thirty years of experience in the field. Operating out of what is essentially a two-car garage, he has become a prominent name in the sport; his chassis are used throughout the sprint car world and by top drivers on the World of Outlaws circuit. A standard Trostle chassis costs approximately $4,000 and contributes only 155 pounds toward a race-ready sprinter's weight of approximately 1,450 pounds.

Previous page
A peek inside the Trostle garage provides a glimpse of the "old school." It is a small workshop crammed to the eaves, with the tools, equipment and memorabilia that comes from three decades of building and racing sprinters. The car in this picture is the house machine, a practice which Trostle has maintained from the beginning of his racing activities. Trostle typically attends seventy races per year, including an annual seven-week trip to Australia during which he sells a number of chassis.

Bob Trostle, a fifty-three-year-old automotive machinist by profession and a highly respected chassis builder by vocation, is an innovator known for the high-quality workmanship befitting a machinist. He was the first major builder to give Jan Opperman a ride in sprinters. The year was 1968 and the car Opperman drove embodied a chassis other drivers of the day found unacceptable. Standard car design had the engine's rear edge mounted on or slightly ahead of a center point between the front and rear axles. Trostle's new chassis had the engine's rear edge approximately eight inches behind the wheelbase midpoint. This positioning, coupled with the car's rear end mounted forward of its normal location, resulted in a chassis that handled very differently from the norm. Opperman, with virtually no experience in a sprinter, simply took the car and did his best with it. His best resulted in an IMCA feature win, in only his second weekend in a sprinter—in a car that no one thought would work. Opperman was on his way and Trostle had permanently altered the thinking about the basic configuration of the sprint car. Constructors soon settled on a five to six inch set-back which, with the advent of aluminum engines, gradually crept back to near the original chassis midpoint.

Next page
In contrast to the Trostle operation, Challenger Racing illustrates a bigger company's approach to building and sponsoring sprint cars. Located in Iowa, Challenger employs approximately twenty people and, like its counterpart, Gambler Competition in Hendersonville, Tennessee, it aggressively advertises and promotes its products.

Much like a modern wholesaler, Challenger keeps a large supply of chassis components in a well-organized and efficiently administered inventory. Standard replacement parts are only twenty-four hours away for the owner of a damaged Challenger chassis.

Next page
Final assembly and check-out at Challenger. Shown here are the cars of Sammy Swindell and Johnny Herrera undergoing final prep for upcoming events.

Personalities

Doug Wolfgang, Sioux Falls, South Dakota. The third winningest driver in World of Outlaws history. Wolfgang is an excellent example of a driver who started racing modified stock cars on local tracks and progressed to being a recognized top competitor in the sprint car ranks. Generally regarded as one of the smoothest drivers on the long half-mile tracks, Wolfgang confines most of his racing to the Pennsylvania circuit and the Midwest area.

Left

Ron Shuman, Tempe, Arizona. A serious money driver, with a success record in midgets, sprinters and a variety of other vehicles. Regarded by many as a cushion rider, Shuman shows no distain for wrenching his car before an evening's racing action.

Bobby Allen, Hanover, Pennsylvania. The complete racer, he builds his own chassis and engines, drives his own cars and is known for driving the low, tight line around a track. Allen started out racing karts, achieving world kart champion status before advancing to sprinters. He appears laid back and easy going, but is regarded by most as a very calculating individual.

Brad Doty, Fredericksburg, Ohio. Not known for having an overabundance of good luck in recent years, Doty is viewed as one of the up-and-coming young lions of the sport.

Team owner, Leonard McCarl and driver Jimmy Sills are caught checking out both the competition and the ever-changing track surface. Sprint car racing, maybe more than any other type, requires that both driver and mechanic be intimately aware of changing track conditions as qualifying, heat races and feature races are run. Drivers and mechanics walking the track they are about to broadside at 100 mph only minutes later is a unique part of the sport.

Steve Kinser, Bloomington, Indiana. An athlete whose accomplishments range from all-state wrestling honors to seven-time World of Outlaws champ. He is regarded by many as the hardest-working driver on the circuit and known for his ability to maintain a consistently high level of effort. Teamed with his relative and car owner Karl Kinser, the combination is probably the most consistently difficult pair to beat on the World of Outlaws circuit.

The calm before the storm Driver John Stevenson spends a brief moment in peace, before the chaos begins. Sprint car racing is exactly as the term implies: an all-out, dog-eat-dog race of short duration. Fifty laps on a half-mile track is a long sprint car race; eight- and ten-lap heat races comprise the majority of an evening's racing. Pacing one's self and car is virtually out of the question. Each competitor is a rabbit: It's the 100 yard dash in track, the fast break in basketball, and the up ice sprint in hockey all rolled into one. Blink once or bobble the car just a little and your chances of winning are gone for good. Rest when you can because once the action starts it's either 100 percent intensity or you might as well be in the stands.

Accidents

100

Previous page
The intention of this photo was simply to catch a group of four cars in close competition in turn one of an important race. The outcome was unexpected. The second-position car in the foursome has just touched the car ahead, snapped around 180 degrees and is about to start a wild tumbling act.

Between the start and finish, the sprinter was nearly six feet off the ground where it hit the fence, punching through two-inch-thick hardwoods as though they were mere toothpicks.

The result of the tumble: All body panels are gone, both wings are torn off, the radiator is lying on the track, the engine is spilling its fluids, the chassis looks heavily bent, yet the driver remains protectively strapped inside the car.

On its way off the racing surface, with oil-dry in the background, you can see the devastation of the chassis. The fuel tank was torn from the car and the rear frame tubes were badly bent. Note, though, how the roll cage remains relatively undamaged.

As mentioned earlier, wings certainly have their opposition. But almost everyone agrees a wing absorbs a great deal of energy and acts to substantially cushion and slow a sprinter that is turned upside-down. It's not hard to see, however, why a crumpled wing can make rapid escape from a damaged car difficult.

On track

Previous page

Here, Steve Kinser is being pushed off for qualification, to the delight of fans at Cedar Lake Speedway near Somerset, Wisconsin. A wet, slippery track, wide tires, lightweight cars and high-compression engines (13:1 is standard) make the push-start more than a simple formality.

While the World of Outlaws has no minimum weight requirement, the typical sprinter weighs about 1,450 pounds and has a wheelbase of not more than eighty-nine inches. With nearly 700 hp, the power-to-weight ratio and short wheelbase make for a very nimble, sensitive combination.

A lone Ford-powered car, driven here by Jeff Swindell. The chassis is a Challenger unit built in Bondurant, Iowa. The upper frame tubes had to be widened slightly in order to drop the wider Ford Windsor block into its proper position.

With the exception of top and front wings, the World of Outlaws prohibits any other airfoils or ground effects devices. In general, sprint car racing has not seen a similar rate of technical advancement found in other forms of racing competition. The surfaces the cars run on have much to do with this. Purposeful rule making designed to keep the cost of racing low has been another reason for limited evolution.

A sprinter engine in trouble. With luck, the problem might only be an oil leak which will be easily corrected.

Shown here is Shane Carson, a regular on the World of Outlaws circuit. An early motorcycle racer before getting involved in sprinters, Carson also promotes sprint car races in his hometown, near Oklahoma City.

Previous page
The back stretch at Knoxville, as a pack of sprinters jockey for the starting flag one-half lap ahead. The infighting through turns three and four prior to the start of a race is often every bit as intense as just after the flag is dropped.

Thankfully for both car owners and mechanics, the day of open-injector stacks protruding through the hood, collecting dirt as well as air, are gone. Upper cylinder wear on valves, rings and cylinder walls was a constant problem. Modern hood design (as shown here on car number 43, with room for large, low-restriction air filters) has done much to preserve engine life and justify spending $20,000 or more on highly refined racing engines.

Sammy Swindell's brand-new Challenger sprinter waiting to run its first laps at Knoxville in August of 1986. Regarded by many as the best natural talent on the World of Outlaws circuit, Swindell is a sprint car pilot who is actively working for Indy car rides. Swindell experienced bad luck with this car during its first outing when the front mounts on the top wing failed, resulting in not only a loose wing but almost no forward visibility on a track filled with high-speed competitors.

Next page
Commercial sponsorship of a team is almost a must if cars and drivers expect to travel a national race circuit. The World of Outlaws pays a towing fee of up to $75 to the top fifteen cars in the standings, but that obviously won't cover expenses. Here we see a trio of sprinters in the late afternoon sun, sponsored by Justice Brothers, an automotive chemical producer.

Doug Wolfgang warms up his sprinter for an evening's races. A mechanically oriented driver, Wolfgang is a professional racer who involves himself deeply in the construction, maintenance and tuning of his car.

Next page
The good old days? While taken in recent times, this photo provides possibly a more realistic look at the past than might be realized: sandy, poor-quality racing surfaces; rooster tails of blinding dust; spectator fences of little value; cars with little driver protection; and drivers so loose in the seat they could lean out the cockpit.

Sprint cars were never known for their comfort. This photo displays the unpadded wraparound driver's cage, contour knee/shin padding below the steering wheel and right-side metal panel for deflecting chunks of clay hurled with numbing force by opposition cars.